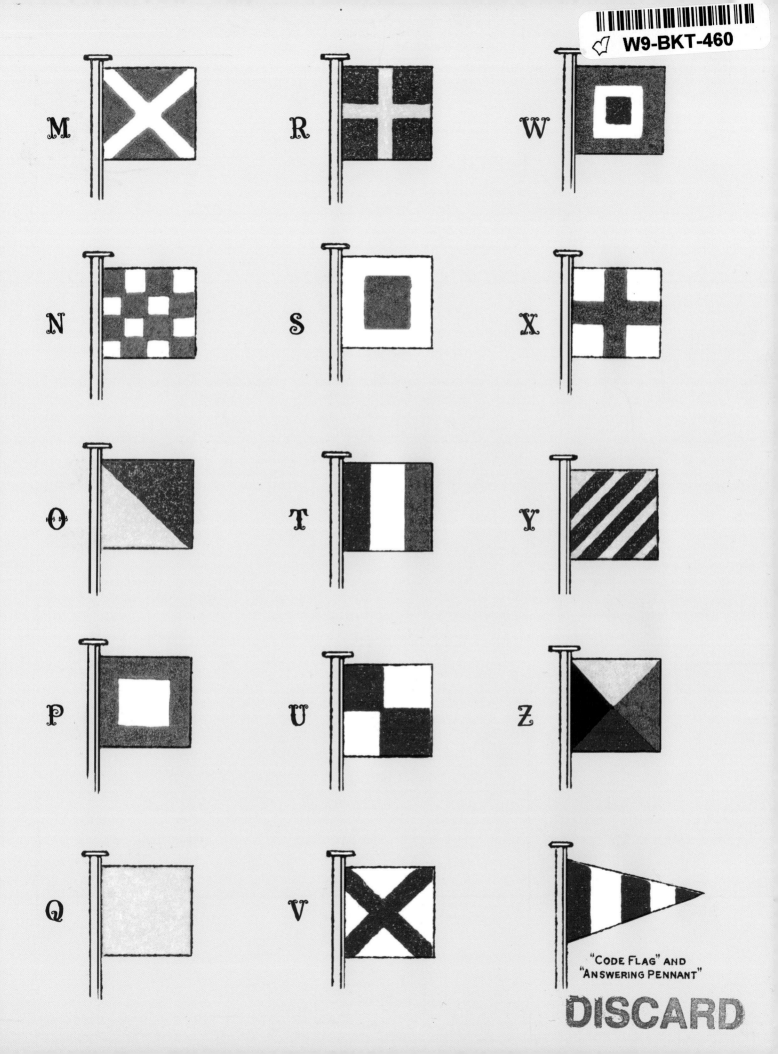

M

R

W

N

S

X

O

T

Y

P

U

Z

Q

V

"Code Flag" and
"Answering Pennant"

Book design by Sara Gillingham.
Text by Shoshanna Kirk.
Manufactured in Hong Kong.

Library of Congress Cataloging-in-Publication Data
T is for tugboat : navigating the seas from A to Z.
p. cm.
ISBN 978-0-8118-6094-9
1. Navigation—History—Encyclopedias.
2. Naval history—Encyclopedias. I. Title.
VK15.T3 2008
623.8—dc22
2007018333

10 9 8 7 6 5 4 3 2 1

Chronicle Books LLC
680 Second Street
San Francisco, California 94107

www.chroniclekids.com

IMAGE CREDITS:

Front cover: tugboat illustration: © 2008 by Grady McFerrin; flag illustration: Dover Publications; float and porthole photos: iStockphoto. Endpapers: Bygone Designs. Page 6: Anchor: iStockphoto; Aground: The Print Collector/Heritage-Images; Ahoy: © Bettmann/CORBIS. Page 7: Buoy: Bygone Designs. Page 8: Canoe: Dover Publications; Captain: Dover Publications; Compass: iStockphoto. Page 9: Dhow: Dreamstime; Dixie Cup: iStockphoto; Dragon boat: © 2008 by Grady McFerrin. Page 10: Even keel: © 2008 by Grady McFerrin; Endurance: © Royal Geographical Society; Ensign: Bygone Designs. Page 11: Float: iStockphoto; Figurehead: iStockphoto; Fireboat: The Mariners' Museum, Newport News, VA; Page 12: Gale: iStockphoto; Gondola: © Historical Picture Archive/CORBIS; Galley: © National Maritime Museum, London. Page 13: Hardtack: © National Maritime Museum, London; Hornpipe: Dreamstime. Page 14: Iceboat: The Mariners' Museum, Newport News, VA; Icebreaker: © Charles Swithinbank/Royal Geographical Society; Ironclad ship: North Wind Picture Archives. Page 15: Jaunty: Dover Publications; Junk: The Mariners' Museum, Newport News, VA; Pages 16–17: Bygone Designs. Page 18: Life preserver: iStockphoto; Lighthouse and "Land ho": Dover Publications. Page 19: Motorboat: The Mariners' Museum, Newport News, VA; Page 20: Neptune: Dover Publications; Navigate: © 2008 Key Color/Index Stock Imagery, Inc.; Niña, Pinta, Santa Maria: North Wind Picture Archives. Page 21: Ocean liner: Dover Publications; Old Salt: The Mariners' Museum, Newport News, VA; Outboard motor: Bygone Designs. Pages 22–23: Paddleboat: Bygone Designs; Pirate and Propeller: Dover Publications. Page 24: Queen Elizabeth: The Mariners' Museum, Newport News, VA; Queen Mary: Advertising Archives. Page 25: Regatta: Bygone Designs; Rowboat: © 2008 by Riley McFerrin. Page 26: Steamship: Bygone Designs; Submarine: iStockphoto. Page 27: Sextant: Dover Publications; Square-rigger: iStockphoto. Page 28: Titanic: The Print Collector/Heritage-Images; Tugboat © 2008 by Grady McFerrin. Page 29: Utility boat: United States Coast Guard; boat illustration © 2008 by Grady McFerrin. Pages 30–31: Flemming Bau/The Viking Ship Museum, Denmark. Page 32: Walk the plank: Bygone Designs; Wheel: iStockphoto; Winch: The Mariners' Museum, Newport News, VA. Page 33: X marks the spot and Skull and crossbones: iStockphoto. Page 34: Yacht: Bygone Designs; Yawl: The Mariners' Museum, Newport News, VA. Page 35: Zephyr: iStockphoto.com; Zodiac: © 2008 by Riley McFerrin; Zulu: © Moray Council (The Falconer Museum), licensor www.scran.ac.uk. Pages 36–37: © 2008 by Riley McFerrin.

T IS FOR TUGBOAT

Navigating the Seas from A to Z

chronicle books · san francisco

Anchor

a heavy object used to keep a boat from floating away

"AHOY!"

how sailors sometimes say hello

Aground

when a boat gets stuck on land

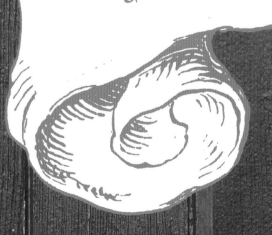

Buoy

a floating object that warns
sailors of danger and helps
them find their way

"Blow the Man Down"

a song sung on a ship

Come all ye young fellows that follows the sea,
To me, way-aye, blow the man down!
Now please pay attention and listen to me,
Give me some time to blow the man down!

B

Canoe

a long, narrow boat rowed
with short paddles

Compass

a simple device that
tells sailors which way
they are going

Captain

the person in charge
of a ship

D

Dixie Cup
a sailor's cap

Dhow
a boat with slanted triangular sails, often sailed on the Indian Ocean and the Red Sea

Dragon boat
a long, narrow Chinese rowboat with a dragon head at the front

E

Even keel
when a boat is level
in the water

KEEL

Endurance
the ship that explorer
Ernest Shackleton sailed
to Antarctica in 1914

Ensign
a national flag flown at sea

Figurehead
a wood carving
at the front of a ship

Float
a device that keeps fishing
nets and traps from sinking

Fireboat
a boat that's like a fire engine
on the water

Gale

a strong wind that creates
rough waves at sea

Gondola

a flat-bottomed Italian boat
rowed by a gondolier

Galley

a ship's kitchen

G

H

Hornpipe
a sailor's dance

Hardtack
a biscuit sailors eat that
can be stored for up to
five years

"HEAVE HO!"
what sailors shout when
they pull a rope

I

Icebreaker

a ship that can break
through ice

Iceboat

a sailboat that travels
over the ice instead of
in the water

Ironclad ship

a wooden ship covered
with iron armor

Jaunty

when a ship is in top
condition, dressed in flags

Junk

a Chinese sailboat

J

Knots
tied by sailors

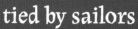

**BIGHT OR
SIMPLE LOOP**

**SIMPLE, SINGLE, OR
OVERHAND KNOT**

**FIGURE-OF-EIGHT OR
GERMAN KNOT**

GRANNY KNOT

**SQUARE KNOT OR
REEF KNOT**

BOAT KNOT

DOUBLE KNOT

SHEEP SHANK KNOT

BOWLINE KNOT

**SHEET-BEND, BECKET-BEND,
SINGLE-BEND OR WEAVER'S KNOT**

SHEET BEND WITH TOGGLE

SINGLE CARRICK BEND

STEVEDORE KNOT

**STEVEDORE KNOT
BEFORE DRAWING TIGHT**

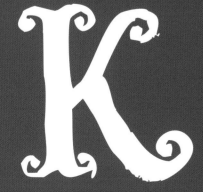

SINGLE BOW KNOT

DOUBLE FLEMISH LOOP

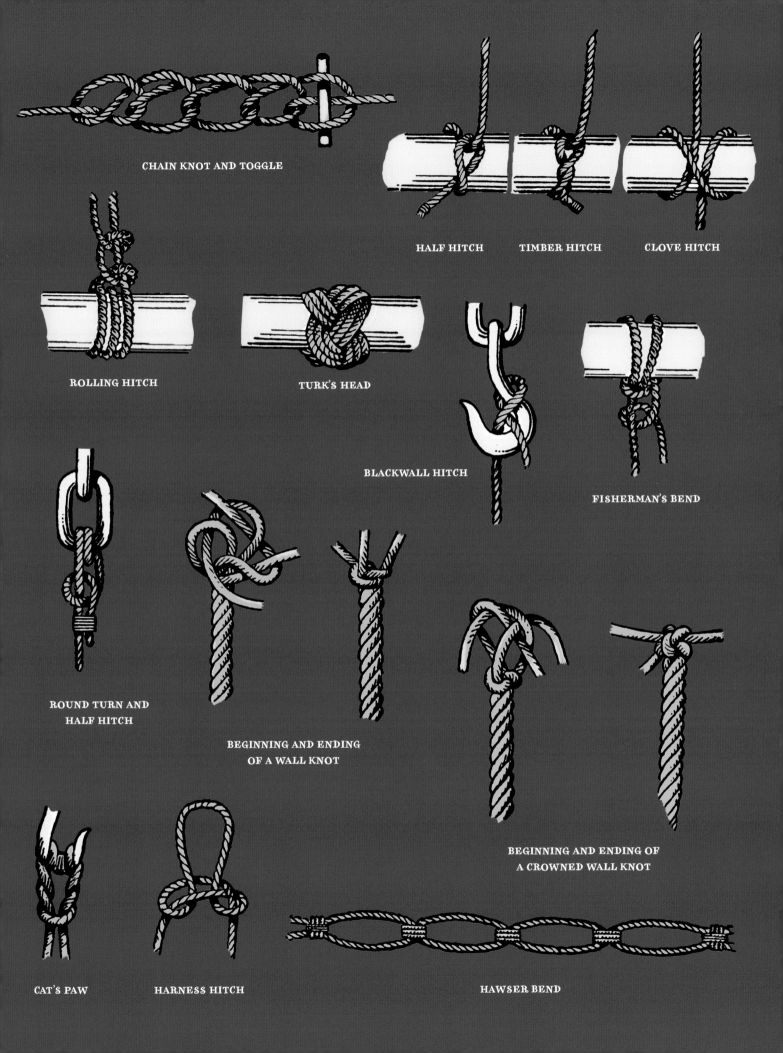

CHAIN KNOT AND TOGGLE

HALF HITCH   TIMBER HITCH   CLOVE HITCH

ROLLING HITCH

TURK'S HEAD

BLACKWALL HITCH

FISHERMAN'S BEND

ROUND TURN AND
HALF HITCH

BEGINNING AND ENDING
OF A WALL KNOT

BEGINNING AND ENDING OF
A CROWNED WALL KNOT

CAT'S PAW   HARNESS HITCH   HAWSER BEND

L

Life preserver
an air-filled tube or vest that keeps people afloat

Lighthouse
a tall tower that flashes a light to keep ships from sailing too close to the shore

"LAND HO!"
what sailors cry when they spot land

Motorboat
a fast boat powered by a motor

A	·—	H	····	O	———	U	··—
B	—···	I	··	P	·——·	V	···—
C	—·—·	J	·———	Q	——·—	W	·——
D	—··	K	—·—	R	·—·	X	—··—
E	·	L	·—··	S	···	Y	—·——
F	··—·	M	——	T	—	Z	——··
G	——·	N	—·				

Morse code
a code of dots and dashes that ships use
to communicate with each other

M

Neptune

the Roman god of the sea

Navigate

to use a map to get
to your destination

Niña, *Pinta*, and *Santa Maria*

the three ships Christopher Columbus
sailed in 1492 from Spain to America

Ocean liner
steamship for carrying passengers on long ocean voyages

Old Salt
a wise, experienced sailor

Outboard motor
a motor mounted at the back of a small boat

Paddleboat

a boat that has a wheel with
paddles to make it go

Pirate

a robber who steals things
from ships

Propeller

rotating blades that
make a boat move

Queen Elizabeth and *Queen Mary*

two English ocean liners built for cruising across the Atlantic Ocean

Quarters

the rooms on an ocean liner where people sleep

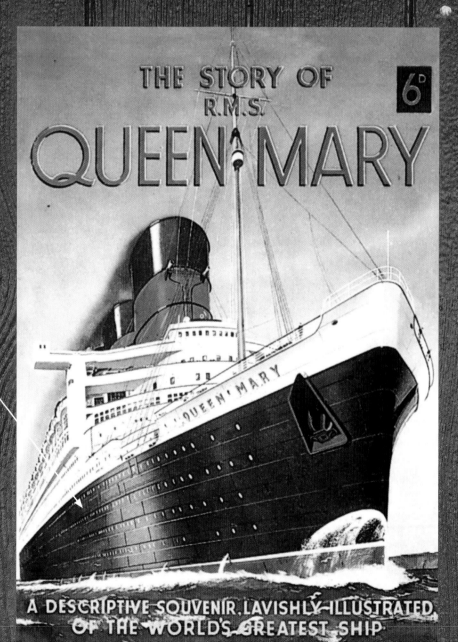

THE STORY OF
R.M.S.
QUEEN MARY

6D

A DESCRIPTIVE SOUVENIR LAVISHLY ILLUSTRATED
OF THE WORLD'S GREATEST SHIP

R

Regatta
a boat race

Rowboat
a boat rowed with oars

Steamship

a ship that moves by steam instead of sails

Submarine

a boat that can go underwater

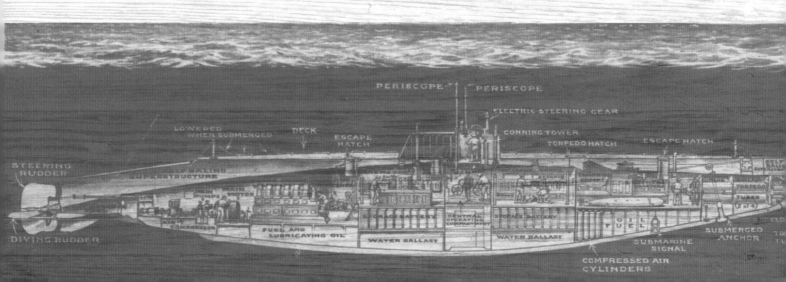

Sextant

an instrument that helps sailors
use the stars to navigate at sea

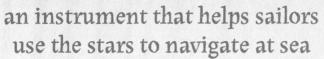

Square-rigger

a ship with square sails

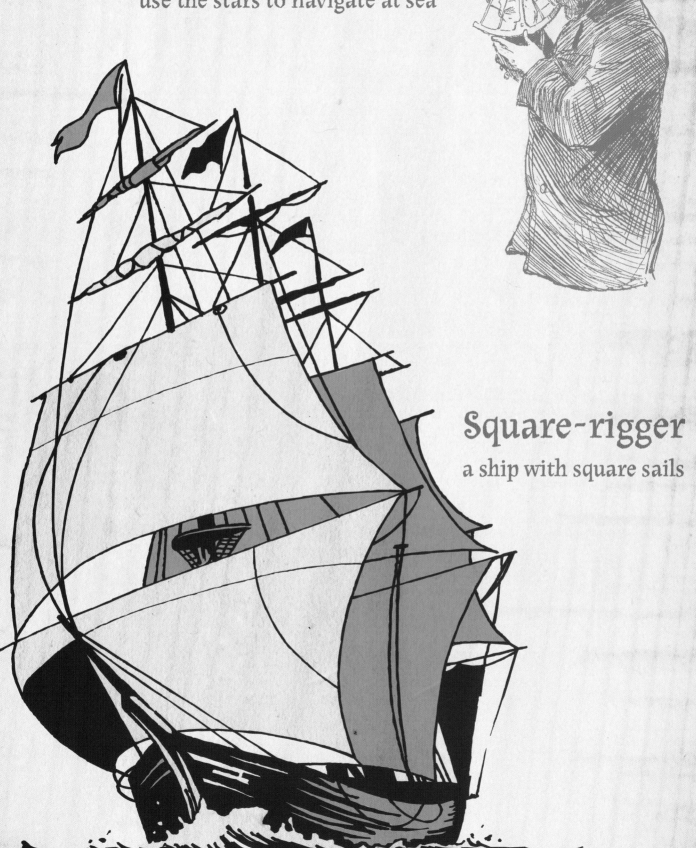

Titanic

an ocean liner that hit an
iceberg and sank in 1912

Tugboat

a small boat that pulls
or pushes other boats

U

Utility boat
a Coast Guard rescue boat

"UP ANCHOR!"

the command shouted
by sailors to pull up an
anchor and set sail

V

Vikings

fierce explorers from Norway,
Sweden, and Denmark who
sailed huge, impressive ships

Walking the Plank

Walk the plank
to be forced by pirates to walk
off a board and into the sea

Winch
a machine that pulls
the ropes that raise and
lower a ship's sails

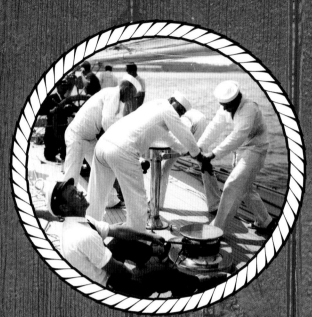

Wheel
used to steer a boat

W

X

X marks the spot— of a pirate's buried treasure

Skull and crossbones
Can you see the X on the pirate flag?

Y

Yacht

a sailboat or a motorboat raced or cruised for pleasure

Yawl

a sailboat with a second small mast for balancing and steering

"YO, HO, HO!"

a pirate's happy exclaim

Zephyr
a gentle breeze

Zodiac
a boat filled with air
often used in the Arctic
and Antarctic Oceans

Zulu
a Scottish fishing boat

Z

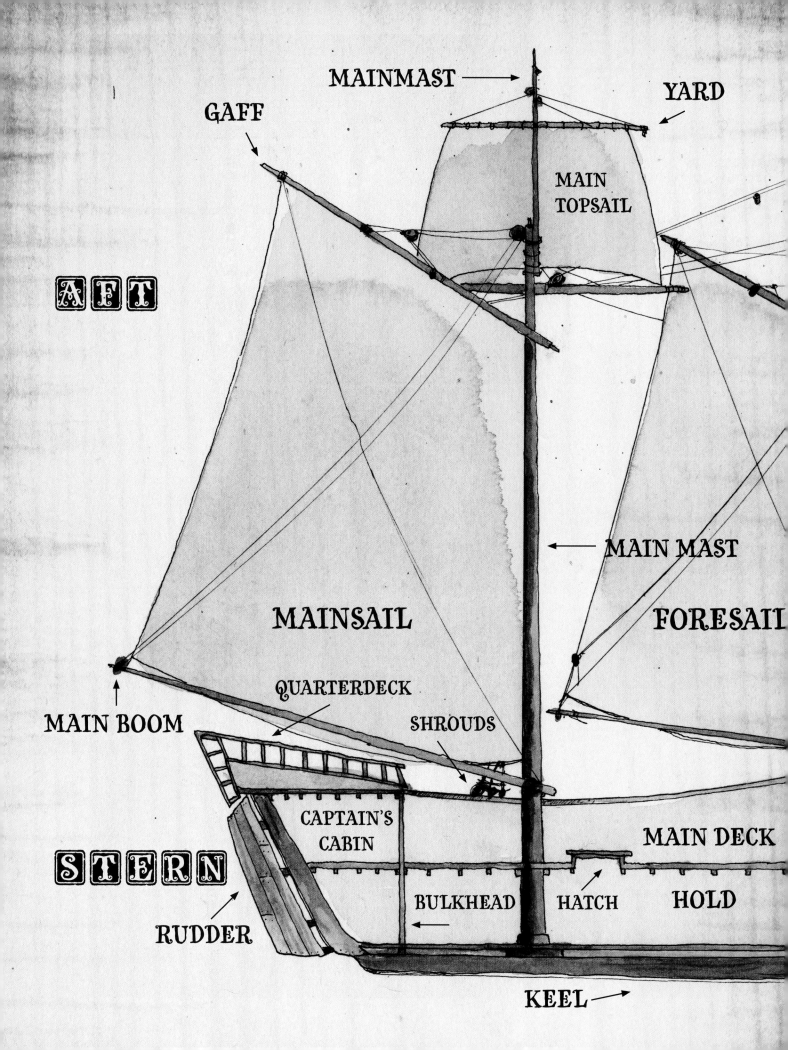

MAINMAST

YARD

GAFF

MAIN
TOPSAIL

AFT

MAIN MAST

MAINSAIL

FORESAIL

QUARTERDECK

SHROUDS

MAIN BOOM

CAPTAIN'S
CABIN

MAIN DECK

STERN

BULKHEAD

HATCH

HOLD

RUDDER

KEEL

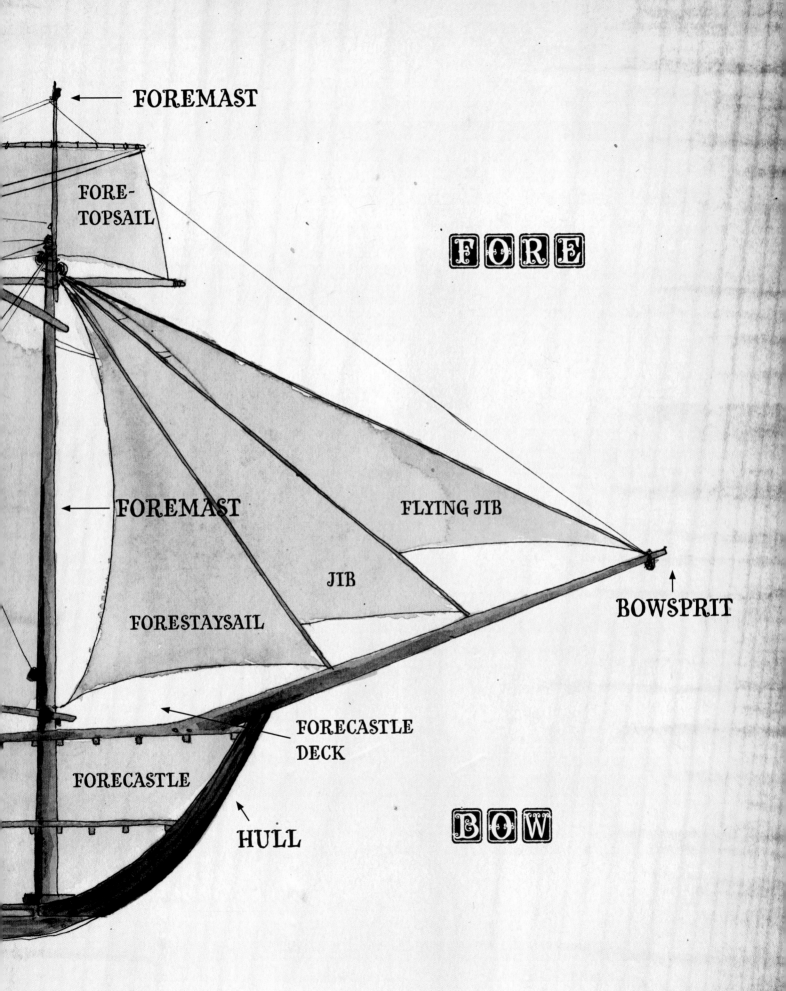

FOREMAST

FORE-
TOPSAIL

FORE

FOREMAST

FLYING JIB

JIB

FORESTAYSAIL

BOWSPRIT

FORECASTLE
DECK

FORECASTLE

BOW

HULL

INTERNATIONAL CODE OF MARITIME FLAGS

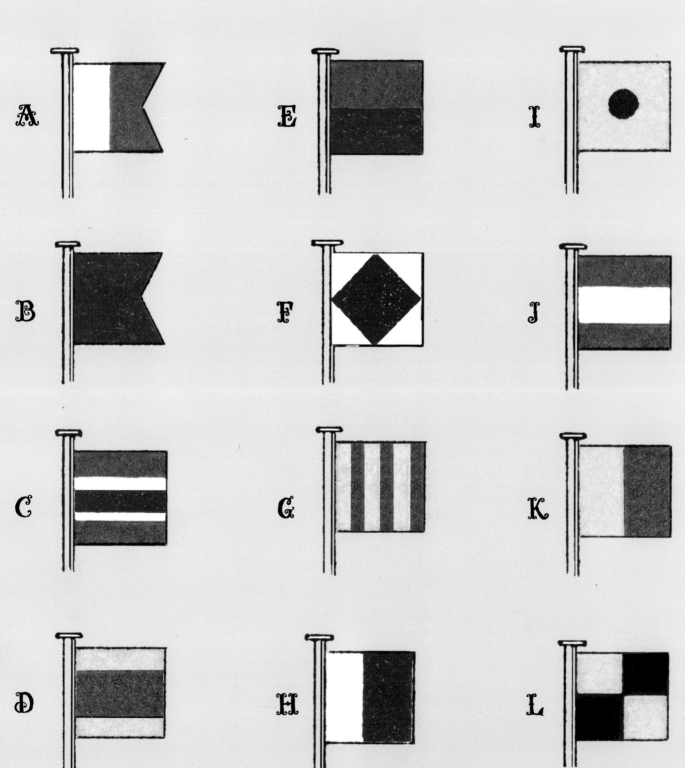